THE OXFORD PIANO METHOD

MORE PIANO TIME CLASSICS

arranged by

Pauline Hall

CONTENTS

(contd.)

Whether we've heard them on recordings, radio, or TV, we all have favourite classical tunes which we'd really like to play if only they were written for the piano. With the 38 really easy arrangements in *More Piano Time Classics*, you'll have an orchestra at your fingertips to play everything from concerto themes to opera arias. With a repertoire of music like this to perform to your friends and family, playing the piano has never been such fun!

P.H.

Illustrations by John Taylor

OXFORD
UNIVERSITY PRESS

Great Clarendon Street, Oxford OX2 6DP, England
198 Madison Avenue, New York, NY10016, USA

Oxford is a registered trademark of Oxford University Press

© Oxford University Press 1995

'Autumn' from The Four Seasons

This is one of the pieces from a set describing the four seasons of the year.

Antonio Vivaldi (1678–1741)

'Bridal March' from the opera Lohengrin

This march, which is often played as the bride enters the church, comes from Wagner's opera *Lohengrin*.

Richard Wagner (1813–83)

Roses from the South

The melody here is in the left-hand part. The accompaniment
needs to be played very quietly.

Johann Strauss (1825–99)

Clarinet Concerto (2nd movement)

Wolfgang Amadeus Mozart (1756–91)

Plaisir d'Amour

Giovanni Battista Martini (1706–84)

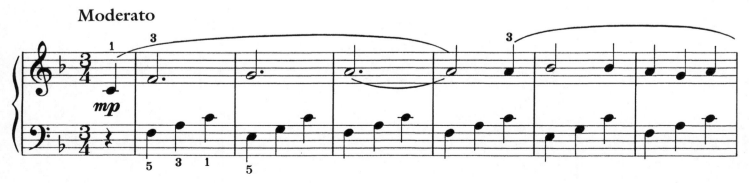

Aria from the opera Orfeo ed Euridice

The myth of Orpheus and Eurydice has fascinated many composers down the centuries. Other composers who have set the story to music include Monteverdi, Haydn, and Offenbach.

Christoph Willibald von Gluck (1714–87)

Largo

George Frideric Handel (1685–1759)

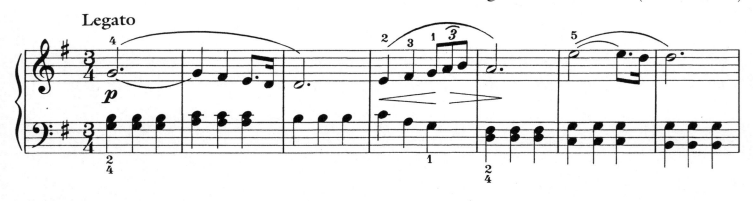

Canon

The word 'canon' means 'rule'; when a piece is called a canon it means that it obeys the rule of 'follow-my-leader'. Can you count how many times the right and left hand melodies of the opening four bars are repeated as a 'canon' through the piece?

Johann Pachelbel (1653–1706)

Sonata Pathétique (2nd movement)

Ludwig van Beethoven (1770–1827)

Tritsch Tratsch Polka

Johann Strauss, famous as a composer of many wonderful and well-known waltzes, polkas, and marches, is often referred to as 'the Waltz King'.

Johann Strauss (1825–99)

La Paloma

A habañera is a slow Cuban dance. It became very popular in Spain.

Sebastian Yradier (1809–65)

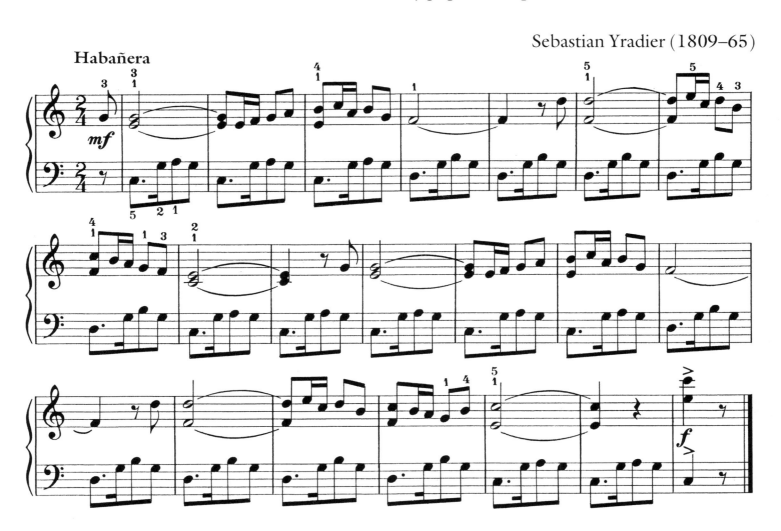

Cradle Song

Franz Schubert (1797–1828)

Prélude from the Te Deum

Marc-Antoine Charpentier (c.1636–1704)

Maestoso

Theme from Sonata K. 331

This is the theme Mozart used for a set of six variations. The original is in the key of A major.

Wolfgang Amadeus Mozart (1756–91)

14

'Dido's Lament' from the opera Dido and Aeneas

This beautiful aria is written over a 'ground bass'; that is, a short melody in the bass which is repeated again and again with changing upper parts. You can hear this bass melody on its own in the first four bars.

Henry Purcell (1659–95)

Slowly, with feeling

*Those with smaller hands can play the last four bars in the left hand as follows:

Marche Militaire

Franz Schubert (1797–1828)

Gavotte

A 'gavotte' is an old French dance in 4/4 time. It always begins on the third beat of the bar.

William Boyce (1710–79)

Minuet in G

Ludwig van Beethoven (1770–1827)

'Morning' from Peer Gynt

This is one of the twenty-three pieces Grieg wrote as incidental music for Ibsen's play *Peer Gynt*.

Edvard Grieg (1843–1907)

'Polovtsian Dance' from the opera Prince Igor

Borodin was in fact a chemist by profession and only composed in his free time. He worked on his opera *Prince Igor* for eighteen years, but unfortunately didn't manage to finish it before his death in 1887.

Alexander Borodin (1833–87)

O for the wings of a dove

Felix Mendelssohn (1809–47)

21

'Romance' from Eine Kleine Nachtmusik

This piece, which means 'A little night music', is a nocturne in four
movements. The original manuscript, recovered in 1955, reveals
that a fifth movement was torn out.

Wolfgang Amadeus Mozart (1756–91)

Waltz from the ballet Coppelia

Léo Delibes (1836–91)

Allegretto grazioso

Trumpet Voluntary

This Trumpet Voluntary wasn't in fact written for trumpet at all, but for the organ!
For many years, it was thought to have been written by Henry Purcell, but it is
now known to be by Jeremiah Clarke who lived at about the same time.

Moderato

Jeremiah Clarke (1670–1707)

The organist would put in trills everywhere the symbol *tr* occurs. If you
would like to add them, they should be played:

'La Réjouissance' from the Fireworks Music

The *Fireworks Music* was written for and played at a royal
fireworks display in London in 1749 to celebrate the Peace of
Aix-la-Chapelle. 'La Réjouissance' means 'rejoicing'.

George Frideric Handel (1685–1759)

Waltz from the ballet Sleeping Beauty

Your right and left hands take it in turns to play the tune (the left
hand starts). The hand playing the accompaniment must play softly.

Pyotr Ilyich Tchaikovsky (1840–93)

Tempo di valse

'Rondeau' from Abdelazer

Henry Purcell (1659–95)

Waltz from the ballet Swan Lake

Pyotr Ilyich Tchaikovsky (1840–93)

Tempo di valse

Dreaming

This comes from a set of piano pieces called *Scenes of Childhood*.

Robert Schumann (1810–56)

Rule, Britannia!

This song has become very popular with audiences at The Last
Night of the Proms in the Royal Albert Hall.

Thomas Arne (1710–78)

Humoreske

A 'humoreske' is a lively, good-humoured composition.

Antonín Dvořák (1841–1904)

poco rit.

Theme from Quartet Op. 3, No. 5

Joseph Haydn (1732–1809)

Andante

Moonlight Sonata

The nickname of this piano sonata came from a comment made by the nineteenth-century poet Heinrich Rellstab, who said that this movement reminded him of moonlight on Lake Lucerne.

Ludwig van Beethoven (1770–1827)

Golliwogg's Cakewalk

This piece comes from a set of pieces for piano called *Children's Corner*.

Claude Debussy (1862–1918)

'Dance of the Little Swans' from the ballet Swan Lake

Pyotr Ilyich Tchaikovsky (1840–93)

Allegretto

Sicilienne

A 'siciliano' or 'sicilienne' is an old dance originating from Sicily.

Gabriel Fauré (1845–1924)

'Elephant' from Carnival of the Animals

The composer wrote this set of pieces for his friends to play in his
own home. This piece is played by a double bass.

Camille Saint-Saëns (1835–1921)

La Campanella

This piece should sound like its title—a little bell. Liszt arranged the melody for piano from Paganini's violin concerto in B minor.

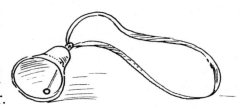

Niccolò Paganini (1782–1840)/Franz Liszt (1811–86)

Reproduced and printed by
Halstan & Co. Ltd., Amersham, Bucks., England